WHEN KITTENS GO VIRAL

Darcy Pattison

Pictures by Nicole Standard

MIMS HOUSE
LITTLE ROCK, AR

For Haileigh, Bruce, Zeke, Gabe, Ash & Neona—
I am so proud of each of you!

Mims House
1309 Broadway
Little Rock, AR 72202
mimshouse.com

Publisher's Cataloging-in-Publication Data

Names: Pattison, Darcy, author. | Standard, Nicole, illustrator.
Title: When kittens go viral / by Darcy Pattison ; illustrations by Nicole Standard.

Description: Little Rock, AR: Mims House, 2020.

Summary: Majestic Kennels, home to the famous cats of KittyTube, welcomes a new star, Angel Persian.

Identifiers: LCCN 2019917048 | ISBN 978-1-62944-142-9 (Hardcover) | 978-1-62944-143-6 (pbk.) | 978-1-62944-144-3 (ebook) | 978-1-62944-145-0 (audiobook)

Subjects: LCSH Cats--Juvenile fiction. | Internet videos--Juvenile fiction. | Online social networks--Juvenile fiction. | Family--Juvenile fiction. | BISAC JUVENILE FICTION / Performing Arts / Film | JUVENILE FICTION / Readers / Chapter Books

Classification: LCC PZ7.P27816 Wh 2020 | DDC [Fic]--dc23

Contents

Other Chapter Books

by Darcy Pattison

THE ALIENS, INC. SERIES

"'Some cats,' Shakespeare said, 'are born great, some achieve greatness, and some have greatness thrust upon 'em.'"

—CLEVELAND AMORY, *The Cat and the Curmudgeon* (1990), opening line

The Persian Kittens

PittyPat—Golden Chinchilla Persian
Angel—White Persian with Odd Eyes
Quincy—Black Persian

A Night of Destiny

— · ★ · —

On a glittering night of destiny, a star was born.

There lay a tiny Persian kitten.

Pure white, she snuggled beside her littermates. Her sister, PittyPat, was a golden chinchilla Persian, who had squawked loudly upon her arrival. But she quickly curled up next to her sister and slept. Quincy was a black Persian, who nosed his sisters with curiosity before falling asleep.

"Grace, are you okay?" asked a gruff voice. That was the Director of Majestic Kennels, a cat who knew something about stars and destiny.

There came a warm purring, purring, purring. "Yes, I'm fine."

The kitten knew that was MamaGrace. The kitten didn't know Gruff Voice and didn't trouble herself about it. Instead, she slept.

The video camera filmed her as she slept, her first screen test for Majestic Kennels.

She stretched clumsily. So adorable.

She rolled over. So sweet.

She yawned.

"Oh! Yowza!" said the gruff voice. "That white one? An angel!"

The name stuck: Angel.

All three kittens were cute.

But Angel? She was a star in the making.

DAY 1
Screen Test

=== · ★ · ===

I yawned and stretched, suddenly awake. Quincy, PittyPat, and I were heaped between MamaGrace's outstretched legs.

A gruff voice said something. I'd heard that cat voice yesterday when it asked if MamaGrace felt okay.

Stanley Sphynx
Director
Majestic Kennels

Now, the gruff voice was purring. It said, "The screen tests are amazing. Yowza!"

"Of course, Stanley," MamaGrace said. "After all, they are my children. And their father was Albert Persian, the Golden Cat."

Stanley smelled like a cat, but not like MamaGrace, or Quincy or PittyPat. He smelled sweet and sharp. He said, "We'll have the videos ready to upload in three days. Do we have permission to put the videos on KittyTube?"

"No." MamaGrace pulled a paw away from us kittens. She reached upward and flinched for some reason. "The kittens must decide."

"They can't decide," Stanley said. "They're too young. Their eyes haven't even opened yet!"

"I know." MamaGrace's voice quivered, and then steadied. "But still I have to ask. And I'll ask the children after every video if they want to do another. If they ever say no, then we'll stop. No matter what."

Stanley's voice thickened. "Yes. We'll ask them after every video. But you have few choices right now. That white kitten—Angel—especially has a chance at becoming a star. If she can act."

I wondered, what was acting?

DAY 2
Family Meeting
=== · ★ · ===

MamaGrace pulled us close to snuggle with her. "Let me tell you a love story." We were two days old. I p-p-purred. "Mama! I can purr."

"Such a clever girl," MamaGrace said. "Do you know what kind of cats purr best? Purr-sians! That's us!"

PittyPat tried to purr, but it came out as a squeak. But Quincy purred!

Quincy and I purred and purred, cozy and comfy.

MamaGrace said, "Enough purring now. I need to tell you about your father."

"Yes!" PittyPat said. "Where is he? When will we meet him?"

"His name is Albert." MamaGrace's voice turned deep as she talked about our father. "He's a tortoiseshell Persian with a red-and-golden coat.

But it's his golden eyes that make him such a great actor. He's got golden eyebrows, a golden chin, and a lovely gold streak down his face."

I put my paw on MamaGrace's leg. The longing in her voice thrummed through me. "You miss him?"

"They called us the Golden Ones. Albert and I were the stars of KittyTube."

"What's KittyTube?" I asked.

"It's our internet channel to show our cat videos. A dozen years ago, a kind inventor gave cats a cat-to-human speech translator. Since then, we've been in control of our videos. We hire human camera operators and film editors and everything else."

I shook my head in confusion. "But what about DaddyAlbert?"

MamaGrace nodded. "Together, Albert and I have over half of KittyTube's overall views. People liked watching us."

Quincy stood and bounced. "Where's DaddyAlbert now?"

"Something happened, and we needed to change jobs. Albert looked for other work. There's a French cat video company called LeChat Carré. That means 'The Square Cat' in French. They promised Albert the lead part in a *Puss and Boots* movie."

I didn't know what videos were, or French, either. Or lead parts or *Puss and Boots*. But it all made

MamaGrace sad. I squirmed closer to her, wanting to comfort her.

"We knew you kittens were coming, so I stayed here. Albert flew to France." MamaGrace's tone turned hard. "But the movie deal fell through. Albert is stranded, with no money to come home."

At her harsh voice, PittyPat, Quincy, and I shivered. We didn't ever want MamaGrace mad at us.

"So, that's it. Albert needs to come home. But we've no money left," she said.

"What's money?" PittyPat asked. "How do we get more of it?"

MamaGrace sighed. For a moment, she was quiet. Her rough tongue caught my cheek. I liked how she cleaned me.

"Money is what we use to buy food. Money pays for everything we do. I used to earn lots of money as an actress. But no more. You can't see me yet," MamaGrace said. "but...I'm ugly."

"Ugly?" That was a strange word.

"A car ran over me last year," she said.

"What's a car?" PittyPat said.

"Later, when your eyes open, I'll show you," MamaGrace said. "For now, all you need to know is this: All our money is gone, spent on hospitals, doctors, and nurses. I limp, my right eye is blind, and my face is scarred. I was a great actress, the best..." Her voice caught, thick with heartache.

I snuggled so hard against MamaGrace that I felt her racing heart. "Mama?"

"It's okay, Angel. I'm okay," she whispered.

I yawned. My eyes were so heavy. I'd been awake for at least fifteen minutes already.

Finally she said, "I was a great actress, but no more." She shook herself, a shiver that went from her ears to the tip of her tail. She stretched taller. "Now I'm a mother, and glad to be so." She gave each of us a quick lick again.

It tickled, so I purred.

"But Albert is stuck in France. We need to bring him home. I'm asking for your help."

Eagerly, Quincy said, "What can we do?"

PittyPat and I repeated together, "What can we do?"

MamaGrace took a deep breath, her chest rising and falling. "You can try acting. The Director—he's the cat in charge of Majestic Kennels—says each of you has a great presence on camera."

"Yes," Quincy said. "Anything to bring our father home."

But PittyPat wanted more information. "What's acting?"

"It's when you pretend to be someone else." MamaGrace explained about video cameras and acting and lots more that I didn't understand. But it didn't matter. If MamaGrace wanted DaddyAlbert home, then I wanted DaddyAlbert home.

In the end, we all said, "Yes."

It was decided. Quincy, PittyPat, and I would try acting. I would be an actress, just like MamaGrace.

I think it was inevitable. We were the children of the top KittyTube stars ever to come out of Majestic Kennels, the Golden Ones.

We were born to act.

I was born to act.

EPISODE 1
Waiting on the Star

=== · ★ · ===

Quincy opened his eyes when he was nine days old, and charmed the world.

The first thing he saw was a ball.

He touched it, and it rolled away. He tumbled after it and tried to bite it.

Quincy batted the ball around for two minutes and thirteen seconds before he got tired. Suddenly he trotted back to MamaGrace, lay down, and went promptly to sleep. His eyes-opening video already had thousands of views.

Today we turned ten days old.

I tried to open my eyes, but my eyelids were stuck fast. I patted at them, but MamaGrace stopped me.

"Don't open your eyes today, Angel," MamaGrace said. "Let PittyPat have her turn."

That was hard. I wanted to act so DaddyAlbert could come home.

When PittyPat opened her eyes, she talked and talked. She looked at something and meowed at it. She patted something else and meowed again. I could listen to her smooth voice for hours.

We hoped for scads of views.

But I wasn't ready for all that.

Let the world wait for this actress.

EPISODE 2
Eyes Wide Open

· ★ ·

I turned eleven days old.

I blinked. The lights shone straight at me.

Oh.

Bright things glared at me. Hard things.

I couldn't smell them. Worried, I shook my head and growled. It came out as a high-pitched squeak.

I stepped backward till my tail touched MamaGrace.

Quincy and PittyPat lay beside MamaGrace. Quincy's eyes-opening video had over 10,000 views. PittyPat's video had thousands of views.

I closed my eyes.

MamaGrace purred and talked at the same time. "No, dear. Keep your eyes open."

I turned to look at her.

"No, dear. Never look away from the camera. Turn around. Let the world get a good look."

I spun around, but too fast. I tumbled to the ground, biting my tongue. Ouch! I swiped a paw across my mouth.

From beyond the lights, a harsh cat voice shouted, "Do that again. Look at your mama, then turn back to the lights and fall down. But don't put a paw across your mouth."

I trembled at the voice. "Who's that, MamaGrace?"

"It's just the Director. See that red light? That means the video camera is shooting. When the red light is on, you do what the Director tells you."

I couldn't see the Director, but I smelled him. Sweet and sharp. And I smelled the human camerawoman too. I looked around at MamaGrace. "I bit my tongue. That's why I wiped my mouth with my paw."

"Does it still hurt now?"

I moved my tongue around. "No."

"Then it's nothing to worry about, dear."

"Why does the Director smell sweet and sharp?"

"He eats peppermint candies. Now do what the Director said. Do it all again but keep your paws off your face."

Quivering, I turned back around to the lights and the Director.

As before, my feet got mixed up, and I fell down.

I looked up and blinked. And blinked. And blinked. The lights dazzled me.

Had I done it right?

"Wonderful!" called the Director. "That's a wrap."

"What's a wrap?" I asked.

"That means you are finished acting for the day," the Director said.

"Good job, Angel," MamaGrace purred.

PittyPat and Quincy said, "Good job, Angel."

The family's purring surrounded me and wound into my heart. I'd done a good job!

"Now come here and snuggle." MamaGrace rolled onto her back.

I lay upon her soft chest, with Quincy and PittyPat beside me.

MamaGrace's heartbeat thumped. I loved her thumping heart.

Someone—the Director—stood beside Mama-Grace. He didn't have soft hair like Mama. He was a hairless cat.

"She's a natural. Yowza! Views will be sky high," the Director said. "And she's going to be a mixed-eye. One blue eye and one copper eye."

What do blue and copper mean? I wondered.

"You can't see her permanent eye color yet," MamaGrace said.

"I can," said the Director. "I know."

Mama purred louder. "Then we have a chance."

"Depends. Poplin Cat Foods is interested in a sponsorship. They'll pay to support KittyTube for six months. But they want a star for the Kitten Adoption Month promotions. Can she do it? Can she become Top Kitten?"

"She'll do it," MamaGrace said. "She has to. We need the money to bring Albert home."

I wanted to listen to the Director. But I was too sleepy.

Purr-r-r-r-r-r.

TALK IT OUT
Work
=== · ★ · ===

I poked Quincy and PittyPat. "What's work?"

"Go away," Quincy mumbled. "I'm sleeping. It's been a long day under the lights."

We were four weeks old now. Every day, MamaGrace took us to a soundstage for acting. I wanted to understand why we had to be actors and actresses.

"You sleep too much," PittyPat told Quincy.

Quincy did a fake snore. "Like I always say..."

PittyPat finished it for him: "...laugh and the world laughs with you. Snore and you sleep alone."

"Exactly," said Quincy. He rolled over and curled up to sleep.

"Let's sit in the sun and talk," I told PittyPat.

We lived in the largest penthouse apartment of Majestic Kennels. It was so big that fifty kittens could've slept there, but it only belonged to my family. Windows looked out over the city in all directions. PittyPat and I liked to sit on the wide windowsill in the sunshine, warm and lazy.

Once, I slept on the windowsill. I woke up often that night to watch the city lights blinking below me. I wondered how many other cats were in the city of Kittywood.

Hollywood, California, was the famous home of the U.S. film industry. Bollywood was the home of film in India. Kittywood was the home of the cats who produce and act in videos. Ever since cats got the cat-to-human-speech translator, the cats controlled all the videos featuring a cat. Kittywood snuggled in a hidden valley in a forgotten part of the U.S. It's home to the five biggest video cat companies:

Majestic Kennels

Cardinal Kennels

Fox Kennels

Wells Brothers Kennels

Malachi-Glenys Kennels

The cats hired humans to film and edit the videos and do other jobs. Groomers kept the stars' coats in shape. Cleaners kept the kennels clean and sweet-smelling. And chauffeurs drove cats here and there.

Kittywood's city parks were planted with catnip, and cat families strolled the streets. It was a city built for cats and those who love us.

"What's work?" I asked PittyPat again.

"Work is when you do what the Director says," PittyPat said. "For us, work is acting in a cat video." She watched me through half-closed eyes.

"But why is it called work?"

"Because we do what the Director asks. Then he lets us live in this penthouse. It's an exchange. We do something for him, and he does something for us."

I thought about that. "He brings MamaGrace food. What if we don't work?"

A shiver went through PittyPat. "MamaGrace is scared of that. If we don't work or if we don't get enough views...well, we'll have to leave. No food and no house."

I thought about that. I didn't want to leave Majestic Kennels. I was learning to act, like DaddyAlbert. I wanted him to come home soon. MamaGrace watched his old videos with us. When he acted, it didn't look like work. It looked like fun.

I did like acting. But I needed to understand it better. Maybe DaddyAlbert could help.

"Do you like acting?" I asked PittyPat.

"Yes!" PittyPat twined her tail around mine. She did that when she was excited. "In my acting videos, I want to surprise people. They think cats will do this or that. I want to do the other things."

Suddenly the door of our kennel opened.

There was the Director.

MamaGrace said he was a sphynx cat. She said he was a fine-looking cat.

But he was bald, and his stomach hung out. His skinny neck was full of wrinkles. His back had rows of wrinkles from his spine to his belly. The only thing not wrinkled was his ears, which were huge.

"Time for work," the Director said.

Quincy sat up and rubbed his eyes. "Yes, sir."

PittyPat bounded toward him, purring, "Yes, sir."

I wished acting made me as happy as it did PittyPat. She knew what she wanted in her videos. Surprises. I didn't know what I wanted. I liked acting and the spotlights and watching the finished videos. I just didn't know what I wanted to do in them.

"Angel!" The Director turned back to me. "Are you coming?"

I sighed. "Yes, sir."

EPISODE 3
Fraidy-Cat

= • ★ • =

The falcon dived down. I leaned against the cold window to watch. I was almost six weeks old and had never seen such a thing.

The falcon's wings were tucked tightly against its side. It went fast, faster, fastest.

My ears twitched.

Pulling up, the falcon grabbed something off the ground. Then it was beating its wings upward.

It landed on the wide ledge outside the window. It opened its claw.

A mouse tumbled out. Small and gray.

"Meow!" My mouth watered.

I wanted to smell the mouse, but the glass was in the way.

The falcon pounced on the mouse.

That falcon was so wild. So dangerous.

I shuddered and turned away, hackles prickling.

"No," the Director called. "Snarl at the falcon."

I wanted to snarl and snap. I knew that would be good acting. I could be a fight cat.

Instead, I stepped backward.

"No," the Director yelled. "Scratch at the window."

I wanted to slash and tear. I knew that would be good fighting.

Instead, I sagged and hid my face under my leg.

MamaGrace said quietly, "It's the fraidy-cat video." She sat behind the lights. I don't work unless she's there.

The Director said, "Hmmm. Maybe."

MamaGrace said, "Every kitten needs a fraidy cat scene."

TALK IT OUT
I Love You

— ⋅★⋅ —

MamaGrace says, "You should always think about the viewer. That's your audience. That's who you act for."

I watched videos of viewers watching videos.

One family that watched viral cat videos made me sad. The video showed a human mama and daughter.

They sat on a couch.

They didn't talk.

The narrator said they never talk to each other. But every day, they watch one cat video together.

It's the only way they can say, "I love you."

I don't understand.

What's so hard about saying, "I love you"?

MamaGrace's Tutorial

=== · ★ · ===

Twenty-seven kittens were born this season across the kennels in Kittywood. That included Quincy, PittyPat, and me. We were six weeks old now.

"You'll give them acting lessons," the Director told MamaGrace.

"No!" Her paw went to the scar on her face.

The Director shrugged and looked around our penthouse apartment. "This doesn't come free. Albert is gone and you can't work in front of the camera. So your kittens act. And you teach."

MamaGrace frowned but finally nodded.

It started a few nights later, after a long day in the sound studio. Twenty-four other kittens crowded into our penthouse, mewling, fighting, and spitting. So many tired kittens were a disaster.

When MamaGrace swept into the room, though, silence descended. Even limping, she moved with a certain grace. A black patch on her right eye blended with the black hair on her face, so that you almost thought she was blinking. Until the second eye never appeared. She might be scarred, but no one could look away.

"Today," MamaGrace said, "we're talking about the different acting roles that cats can have."

PittyPat, Quincy, and I sat on the floor at MamaGrace's feet. The other kittens sank to the floor too. We were learning from the queen, and we knew it.

MamaGrace nodded to Mr. Danny. A large, red-faced man, Mr. Danny was the Director's right-hand man and did anything and everything the Director needed. Mr. Danny turned on the projector and turned out the lights. MamaGrace talked while we watched slides and videos.

"Cat actors and actresses have different roles in their lifetime," MamaGrace said. "These are video clips of some of those roles."

"Innocent cat is a role for young cats, like you kittens. Innocent cats are naive, which means they know nothing. It's funny to watch them mess up everything. All of you have started as innocents. You can't stay there, but that's where you start."

On-screen, DaddyAlbert scrunched his baby face and charmed the camera. As an innocent, he was soft and mellow.

The next slide appeared, and MamaGrace said, "Dress-up cats love to wear crazy clothing. They are feline-fine!"

There was DaddyAlbert wearing cowboy boots in one picture, and in the next, a tuxedo. I'd no idea my daddy was so handsome!

A film clip was next, showing a tiny Siamese cat in a musician's costume. The costume fit onto the kitten's front legs and chest. Sewn onto the costume were miniature human hands that held a guitar. From the front, the cat looked like a miniature person (with a cat face) playing a guitar.

"Jazz, please stand up," MamaGrace said, "and take a bow."

The cat beside me stood. She was about my size—we were both small, even for kittens. Her Siamese face was dark and serious. Bowing, she said, "Thank you, Madam."

Everyone cheered for her, and a smile finally showed up on Jazz's face.

When she sat, the next slide didn't work.

"I'll have to turn on the light to fix it," said Mr. Danny. The human-to-cat speech translator made his voice sound buzzy, like a robot.

While the lights were on, I turned to Jazz. "I'm Angel. That was a great dress-up video. Were your parents dress-up cats too?"

"No. I'm the first video cat in my family. My brother and I auditioned every day for three weeks. Just to get here. My parents really wanted this for us."

"Oh." I realized that I had no idea how outside cats got a chance to act in a video. I only knew about those of us born here. "Well, you were amazing." I wondered if we'd be friends. MamaGrace didn't notice many kittens, so Jazz must be a good actress. I needed good actresses as my friends.

Around us, the kittens meowed and chatted.

Suddenly Jazz leaned toward me. "It must be easy for you. The daughter of the Golden Ones." She looked over at MamaGrace and frowned.

I stepped backward. "No, it's not easy. I work hard."

"Yeah." She waved a paw around. "From the penthouse."

"You don't know anything," I said angrily. "Yes, I live here. But it's hard because my mom was hurt in a car wreck and can't be in videos anymore. DaddyAlbert went to France to look for work and got stranded. MamaGrace cries in her sleep and doesn't even know it."

I put a paw over my mouth, and my eyes grew wide. I hadn't meant to say all of that.

Jazz stepped backward. We were standing so far apart. "I didn't know," she said in a quiet voice.

I took two steps and said into her ear, "Don't you dare tell anyone that she cries."

Mr. Danny called, "Lights out."

I shoved PittyPat toward Jazz and sat between my brother and sister, away from that Siamese. Why had I told Jazz so much about our family? MamaGrace and DaddyAlbert were famous, but even famous people have problems. But why tell Jazz all that? I shook my head. I didn't understand myself.

MamaGrace waved at a new slide and said, "Water cats love anything to do with water."

I nudged PittyPat, who loved water too. She leaned forward to watch the film of Peter Reuben, the master of the water-cat role.

"This is clever editing," MamaGrace said. "Peter was videotaped taking a bath every day for a year. This video puts together his best 100 jumps into a big water bowl—in just 100 seconds. It's a well-known fact that cats hate water. But that's what makes a water cat so popular on KittyTube. It's the unexpected."

That's what PittyPat had said! I nudged her again, and this time she flashed me a smile. PittyPat, the CatFish.

The video raced through the splashing water, while around us the kittens laughed and giggled nervously. Everyone was wondering about their own next role.

Jazz shook her head, and Angel agreed. No water for her.

MamaGrace's voice was hypnotic in the dark. "Chase cats will chase their tails, or shadows or anything else. Albert Persian was a whiz at this. There are classic tricks that you can repeat. You just need a slight new twist. For example, there's the classic chasing-your-tail trick."

We laughed at DaddyAlbert's tail that flowed like a river of gold. He never caught it.

"In the open, the trick looks one way," MamaGrace said. "For variety, try it on carpet, on a wood floor, or on grass. Or you can chase tails in an enclosed place like a bathtub. Or in a bowl or a bathroom sink that just barely fits your body. Or you can chase your neighbor's tail."

DaddyAlbert chased a pretty young cat and caught her tail. I gasped. That was MamaGrace.

"Honey," he said, "I'd die for you!"

"How many times?" Mama Grace said.

And my heart clenched at how beautiful they were together. And how sad it was that DaddyAlbert couldn't get home.

But MamaGrace was already on the next video clip. "Fat cats do normal everyday things, but their size makes the videos funny. Usually, these are older cats. Wesley Maine Coon used to be a chase cat. As an older cat, though, he'll have many more videos as a fat cat."

Wesley towered over the other cats in the video. He wasn't so much fat as just a giant. A mountain of a cat.

"Food cats," MamaGrace said, "will eat anything. Beetles, spiders, shoes, or superhero action figures. My son, Quincy Persian, already loves to eat. Watch."

PittyPat and I pounced on Quincy, who hid his head in embarrassment. But we sat up quickly to watch the video. It opened with Quincy batting around a large garden spider. Finally he pounced and swallowed it. But he didn't use his teeth. He didn't chew.

His face screwed up. He tilted his head.

And then, a spider leg appeared between his teeth.

The audience gasped.

On screen, Quincy bent his head, and then lifted it high, trying to swallow.

He paused. His eyes looked up. Then down.

A moment later, a spider leg appeared again.

Quincy coughed. And that spider crawled out of his mouth.

Oh! In the penthouse, kittens screamed and wailed, scared by the spider that was bigger than life on the video. I turned to watch them and smiled. Quincy had nailed it with his acting. The video editors were brilliant.

On the video, Quincy yowled, "I don't want to be a food cat!"

Now, THAT was a great food cat video. It would get heaps of views.

Mr. Danny flipped on the lights, and MamaGrace was gone.

Instead, the Director stood there. "Today," he said, "I'd like to announce the competition for this season's kittens. Poplin Cat Foods needs a star for Kitten Adoption Month. For the next six weeks, we'll track your views. Whoever has the highest number of views on their videos will be Top Kitten. Poplin has pledged $1,000 to the Top Kitten. Yowza!"

Pandemonium.

That's a big word—I'm learning big words and big ideas now. It means the kittens went crazy. What an uproar, a furor, a hubbub, a ruckus. "I'll be Top Kitten," they all cried.

My heart pounded with excitement. Poplin Cat Foods had agreed to the competition! We had a chance to bring DaddyAlbert home.

In the shadows near the window, MamaGrace wiped a tear from her good eye.

The Director raised a paw. Slowly, the kittens quieted. "Top Kitten right now," he said, "is Jazz, the Siamese kitten, with her musician video."

I turned to stare at Jazz. We didn't understand each other because our families were so different. But still, I'd hoped for a friend. Instead, she was competition. Serious competition. Could she be both a friend and the one to beat?

"Second," the Director said, "is Quincy with his 'Eat the Spider' video. A distant third is Angel Persian with her Fraidy Cat video. For the next six weeks, I'll update weekly scores each Sunday night and post them early on Monday morning."

At least Quincy came in second for Top Kitten this week. Quincy, PittyPat, or I had to be Top Kitten at the end of the contest. Because that's the only way our DaddyAlbert was coming home. But maybe it would be okay if Quincy won, so I could be friends with Jazz. If she wanted to be friends.

Big Words

— ⭐ —

I'm learning big words now.

A group of cats is called a clowder of cats. The word *clowder* dates back to Middle English, about 1800. It comes from a word meaning "clot." *Clot* means a tight group of things. A group of cats could be clotted together.

To remember that a group of cats is called a clowder, try this tongue twister:

"A cluttered clotting cluster of cats creates a clowder."

Odd Eyes

I looked at MamaGrace and then at the Director. MamaGrace blinked her good eye.

The Director jumped up from his red mat, walked around me, and went back to sit down again. Leaning forward, he said, "It's true."

MamaGrace nodded. "She's got odd eyes. One blue and one copper."

"It's a beautiful blue." The Director rose again to come to squint at my eyes. "Aqua blue. Yes, almost sapphire. And the copper is like a shiny penny." He spun around, his skinny body looking like a ballerina's. The image was ruined by his impossibly large ears.

"Will this help her views?" MamaGrace said.

"Help? Oh, yes." The Director tapped the wall chart with the videotaping schedule. "I'll move the schedule around. We need a special video tomorrow to showcase them. Can you coach her acting on how to make use of those gorgeous eyes?"

MamaGrace smiled. And purred.

I rubbed my head against her nose. "Is it good, Mama? Will it help DaddyAlbert come home?"

"Yes, dear. We have a chance."

EPISODE 4
The Eye of the Soul

— ·★· —

"Quiet on the set!" the Director called.

The rustling quieted. I was almost seven weeks old and getting used to the soundstage.

"Lights!"

The bank of lights turned on, blazing.

MamaGrace and the Director disappeared behind the glare.

I blinked.

"Action!"

I blinked and blinked. Blue and copper. Blinking.

I turned around, looked straight at the camera, and meowed.

That's it.

I just meowed.

It was my most woebegone meow.

It was a cry for my mama.

It was a cry for someone to come and pick me up and pet me.

Someone, please. Lonely. Needy. DaddyAlbert, come home.

MamaGrace said my odd eyes were riveting. That means people couldn't look away.

I looked straight at the camera and said, "Mew! Eh!"

The "Eh!" was for an exclamation. It made it sound even sadder.

MamaGrace says that looking into the camera's eye creates a special soul contact.

Me connecting with you.

That scares me.

But it shoots the views sky high.

Meeew! Eh!

The Camera

═ • ★ • ═

After a long day of acting, it was hard to calm down.

PittyPat and Quincy flopped onto a sleeping pad. I paced along the windows, checking top and bottom for cameras. I strode the four walls of the room, looking into each dark corner where a camera might hide. In the room's center, I flipped over sleeping pads, looked under MamaGrace's chaise lounge and Mr. Danny's chair, and finally sat with my head twisting back and forth, searching. My tail twitched and my ears twitched. "Are there any cameras here?" I asked.

Quincy and PittyPat stared at me.

"No cameras," Quincy said. "Are you okay?"

"No cameras," PittyPat said. "Come, sit with us."

I breathed deeply. Maybe I could relax.

I was trying so-o-o-o hard to be Top Kitten so DaddyAlbert could come home.

No cameras. Finally.

I hated being onstage all the time. Acting was still fun, except when it didn't end. Acting every day, all day long—I was tired.

Quincy flopped down on his back, letting his legs stick straight up.

"Teach me that," PittyPat said. She flopped down on her back. But her legs were folded up, relaxed. She looked at Quincy and straightened her legs. "Like that?"

She crossed her front legs. "What about this?"

She stretched her legs on one side but relaxed them on the other side. "Or what about this?"

I didn't want to pose upside down.

I didn't want to meow like a tiger.

I didn't want to meow like an elephant.

I just wanted to be me.

But the camera ruled our lives.

"Smile for the camera," the Director said.

"Action!" the Director said.

The problem was that I watched the camera.

You've heard it said: "It's easy to take a dog's picture. He doesn't pose. He doesn't know the camera is there."

Some days, I just wanted to be a dog.

EPISODE 5
Snow Angel

— · ★ · —

Last night, there was great excitement in Majestic Kennels.

Snow.

It was a late-spring storm. MamaGrace says that most kittens are born in the spring. So it's rare to see a video of a kitten with snowflakes.

That's why my video has already racked up a pile of views.

They woke me up in the middle of the night.

The Director had done snow videos before. He knew how to light the scene. It had to be on the outside set, of course. They just added a dark screen behind me. My odd mixed eyes against that black screen would film well. But I shivered and shivered.

Stretching, I sat and curled my tail around me for warmth.

But MamaGrace said, "No, dear. It's time to work."

You don't tell her no when it's time to work.

I yawned.

"No yawning. Look lively," the Director called.

I stretched and yawned. Slowly, I woke up.

Finally I nodded at the Director. "I'm ready to act."

I walked onto the set. Snow sprinkled across the brown grass. Cold!

"Look up," the Director called. Sometimes he screamed at me, which I hated. But tonight he was quiet. Maybe the snow enchanted him too. I breathed slowly, trying to match his slow breaths.

Looking up, I sat on my back legs in surprise.

Huge, white flakes fell toward me.

One fell toward my face!

I leaped aside, batting at it.

MamaGrace crooned, "Rrruh!" That meant I was doing good acting!

The snowflakes fell soft and gentle.

I played.

I let one snowflake fall onto my tongue. Shiver.

I let one fall onto my blue eye. Blink, blink.

I let one fall onto my copper eye. Blink, blink.

I batted one down. Score!

I snapped at one just above my nose. I missed.

I scooped up snow with my front paws and rubbed my nose in it. Shiver.

Shiver.

Shiver.

"Cut," called the Director. "Well done, Snow Angel."

I love snow.

This was fun acting.

Jazz Is STILL Ahead

=== · ★ · ===

A clowder of kittens pushed and jostled for position. It was the second week of the Top Kitten contest, and everyone wanted to see the scores.

"Stand back," yelled the Director. Mr. Danny, his right-hand man, gently pushed through the clowder to the wall. He taped a piece of paper there and stepped back.

I waited, not caring to shove and push. But PittyPat and Quincy wove through the crowd to the front. PittyPat called loudly, "Top Kitten this week is Jazz, with her 'Monkey Business' dress-up video."

I turned away and stared at the classic posters that lined the front lobby of Majestic Kennels. My favorite was the one that showed DaddyAlbert and MamaGrace dancing together. My second favorite showed them rowing a boat together. Together. Always together. And now they were an ocean apart.

And I hadn't made Top Kitten again. Two weeks gone. Only four left.

"Angel, did you see your score?"

I turned to Jazz and forced out the words. "No. I just heard that you're Top Kitten again this week. Congratulations!"

Jazz sat on her haunches and licked a paw, which meant she was happy with herself.

I covered my jealousy by talking. "You're a really great dress-up cat."

"I definitely do NOT like the monkey outfit," Jazz said. "For the video, they tried to jam a banana down my mouth—yuk! I don't want to be a food cat."

"What amazes me is your costumes," I said. "They're amazing."

Jazz stopped cleaning her paw and stared at me. "Thanks. But why are you being so nice to me?"

I shook my head, puzzled. "I'm not being nice. You're a good actress, and I like your videos."

"You don't think it's weird that I'm a Siamese doing dress-up?"

"No."

"It's so hard!" Jazz said. "I have to be a successful actress, and more important, I have to not embarrass the Siamese world."

"They don't like dress-up?" I said.

"Not at all! I'm a different sort of Siamese, I guess. How can I dress just one way? I love to dress up in different clothes."

She was right. Usually, Siamese don't like to be touched or dressed. Ragdolls might get coddled and dressed up. Not a Siamese.

Quincy walked toward us, but I waved him off. I could find out my ranking after this talk with Jazz.

"Will it matter to your parents if your videos get lots of views?"

"Of course," Jazz said. "I need to be successful so we can stay in Kittywood. We don't want to go back to the normal world of cats."

"This crazy business only works if you're true to yourself."

Jazz nodded. "Your snowflake video showed you as yourself. You weren't acting in that one, were you?"

"Yes and no." I laughed at the memory of the cold snow. "Sometimes I'd turn a certain way or hold a pose for the camera. But mostly I just played with the snowflakes."

"That's why you're so good at this," Jazz said. "You do it naturally."

We stared at each other. I really liked her monkey video, and she really liked my snowflake video. Maybe we could be friends.

"Say," I said, "we were going to the park to play in the Catnip Meadow. Want to come?"

Jazz half closed her eyes, and then turned her head away. "No," she said harshly. "I don't think it's a good idea. Only one of us can be Top Kitten." Then she walked away.

Surprise left me speechless. I had to blink away tears. The competition was important, of course. But was it so important that we couldn't be friends?

TALK IT OUT
The Groomers

—— · ★ · ——

What should you use to comb a cat?

A catacomb!

I held my paw as still as I could until Miss Tanya worked out the tangles.

It was the worst part of my day: grooming.

A dozen cat groomers worked at Majestic Kennels. Each cat was cleaned every day.

But my cotton-white coat was the hardest to groom. My hair had to float for the camera.

Every morning, Miss Tanya worked on my coat for at least an hour. First she used a wide metal comb, moving to a finer comb when the big tangles were out.

Armpits were the worst. Hair under my arms and legs matted easily. A good groomer separated the mat into small sections. Each section was combed by itself until it was straight. Sometimes powder helped the knots come out.

I always liked the powder that smelled like oranges. And I liked to study DaddyAlbert's videos while Miss Tanya worked. He did so many roles that he was a good actor to study. If he were here to teach me, I'd easily be Top Kitten. Of course, if he were here, I wouldn't need to be Top Kitten.

His best role was as a leading man. That means DaddyAlbert was the handsome boy cat who won the heart of the beautiful girl cat. Oh, it was old-fashioned in some ways. But it was his stage presence that caught me. How did he make you care so much? His movements were small. He didn't leap and roll around like Quincy. Sometimes, the camera just caught him standing and looking toward something off-stage. But the moment was deep and emotional. His videos made the grooming time pass quickly.

Grooming was the worst when the matted hair was so bad that it had to be cut out. Miss Nicole did that once. Just once. The Director fired her, and she never came back.

Instead, Miss Tanya came the next day. She's never let my arm pit get matted again.

Here's a big no-no! Yellow or brown stains (no way!) under the eyes or on the ruff, hocks, or rear. Eek!

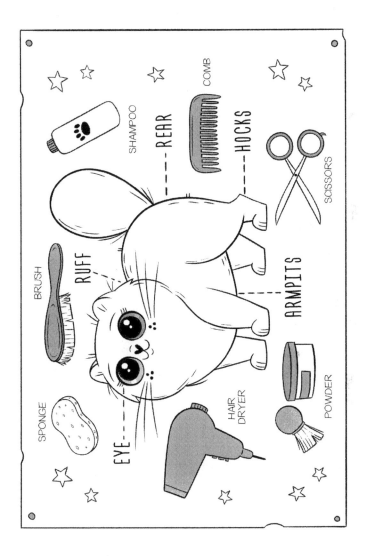

After my fur, my eyes were cleaned. A weather change could make my tears yellow or brown. Miss Tanya dipped beauty sponges in a weak acid. She cleaned one eye at a time. The sponge wiped away any stain.

Finally, after all that, it was time for my daily bath. Miss Tanya used gloves and a special clear shampoo. I hated the baths, getting all wet. So I'll skip over telling that part.

Hair dryers finished the job.

It's hard to look good on camera.

TALK IT OUT
The Mirror
⸻ ·★· ⸻

I look in mirrors all day long.

There's a plain mirror near the door of our apartment.

I like it best because it says, "Hello, Angel. I know who you are."

At the studio, we rehearse stunts in a mirrored room. A rehearsal is just practicing the stunt.

I stand at one spot. There, in the mirrors, I see myself looking at myself six times back.

These mirrors say, "Who are you today?"

PittyPat knows who she is as an actress.

She loves, loves, loves water.

For a cat, that's odd.

Baths. Bubble baths. Falling in. Climbing out.

There's an art to looking charming when your fur is all wet.

It takes great acting.

PittyPat practices looking both upset and gleeful.

She squawked loudly on the night she was born, and she's been using that voice ever since. She sings mournful songs that connect with the viewer's soul. I connect with my mixed eyes, but she connects with her voice.

She hasn't done a spray-hose yet.

Will she like that too?

Or will that make her get out of water-cat videos?

Quincy knows who he is as an actor.

He can eat anything.

Put him in a kitchen with a clumsy cook. He'll lick the spills. Or the cook's face.

Odd foods attract him. Yogurt. Crickets.

One cricket escaped, and they chased it around the studio.

A cameraman filmed it all.

They cut the video down to a 30-second chase.

Great acting!

It's an exciting video! Oodles of views.

Crickets. Yuk. NOT FOR ME.

The mirror tells me, "You're an innocent."

But we're getting older.

PittyPat and Quincy have moved on to other roles.

But I'm still stuck as an innocent.

I need to move on too.

MamaGrace says, "Don't worry. You're still getting heaps of views."

The mirror says, "You can't stay an innocent forever."

I stand at the right place, and six of me look back. All are innocents.

I look at six innocents that look like me.

Inside, I don't feel like an innocent. Innocents are naive and do funny things because they don't know better. I long to do something intelligent.

"Watch me!" I tell the mirror.

I push my claws out.

I show my sharp teeth.

I flatten my ears.

I am wild!

The mirror just laughs at my acting.

Jazz AGAIN

· ★ ·

The third week's list of popular videos was posted amid more pandemonium.

Quincy, PittyPat, and I were not in the top three. I was fourth. PittyPat was eleventh with a new water video. Quincy was seventeenth with a new food-cat video.

Jazz was number one. Again.

What else could we do? What other videos could we do? What other roles?

We couldn't give up. We were already nine weeks old. Soon we'd move to the dormitory with the other kittens. That would leave MamaGrace all alone. That would break my heart. She needed DaddyAlbert.

After seeing the scores, I cried and cried. But then I dried my tears and made a decision. I would study the acting of other cats.

Yes, study.

I needed to learn.

I wanted to be a better cat actress. I needed to be the best! Top Kitten!

Studying Acting

·★·

STUDY: QUINCY'S VIDEO

Food cats like Quincy have odd ways to eat. Chopsticks!

Quincy clutches the chopsticks in one paw. He bites the top of the other chopstick.

He moves slowly, stopping to stare at the camera with coppery eyes.

He moves the top chopstick by turning his head.

He blinks, slowly. He opens his eyes w-i-d-e.

He jabs a piece of meat.

The nugget of meat falls off.

IMPORTANT: Here's what I am learning. Every video is a small story.

In a good story, the main character can't win the first time. They must try it twice and fail. They can only win the third time.

Quincy stabs the meat again.

It works! He lifts the chopstick to his mouth. He opens his mouth.

The meat falls off.

IMPORTANT: Using his body language, Quincy tells the camera that he's mad. He hunches forward. He narrows his eyes. His tail lashes about. He lets his claws come out to clutch the chopsticks. That's good acting.

Quincy tries again. This time, he clutches and bites the chopstick. He pinches meat between the sticks. He takes his mouth off the chopstick. Quick, he leans forward.

The meat falls. Again.

But before it hits the ground, Quincy snatches it up!

Success!

STUDY: PITTYPAT'S VIDEO

PittyPat's green eyes look awesome with her chinchilla gold hair. Chinchilla means she has a golden-colored undercoat. She's creamy white on the chest and shoulders. Her hair is black tipped on the head, back, tail, and legs. Her nose is the most beautiful pink.

(*My nose is red, and Quincy's nose is red.*)

PittyPat is a lovely Persian.

That's why her videos are so shocking!

There she is, trapped on the far side of a bathtub. (No one knows how she got there. She just gets in trouble a lot.)

The bathtub is full of water.

PittyPat hunkers down by the wall, as far from the water as possible.

"Meow," she cries. Her voice is rich and deep. She knows how to use her voice when she's acting!

Her tail swishes back and forth.

CUT to the food bowl.

ACTING WORDS: Each video is a tiny story told by the actor or actress. But it's a story with video. CUT means to suddenly change to a different picture. In PittyPat's video, it cuts from a picture of PittyPat to a picture of PittyPat's food bowl.

CUT back to PittyPat.

IMPORTANT: PittyPat tells the camera that she's hungry with her body language. She sucks in her stomach to look skinnier. She bats at the water. She licks her lips. She voices her hunger with pitiful meows. Great acting!

She's hungry, PittyPat tells the camera.

Starving.

The only thing keeping her from her supper is that bathtub full of water.

Light glares off the white bathtub. There's a strange ripple in the water.

Suddenly PittyPat leaps.

Her legs move frantically.

Doggie-paddling.

(Why don't they call it kitty-paddling?)

Splash, splash!

Splish, splash, splish!

To show how hard it is, she says, "Grrrowl!"

Her voice is scratchy.

The viewer worries about her.

She tries to climb up the slick bathtub.

Oh, no!

She falls back in.

She's under water.

For a long moment, she's under water. (I'm worried.)

She's under water. *(I'm worried more.)*

She's UNDER WATER! *(I'm desperately worried! Making the audience wait like this adds to the emotional depth of the storytelling.)*

There! She's up.

PittyPat says, "Meeeew!"

The cry strikes into the heart. She's trying SO hard!

She slips on the slick bathtub.

She falls in, but this time she keeps her wet slicked-down-hair face above water.

IMPORTANT: This is good storytelling. PittyPat has failed two times.

The wet cat tries to climb up. Her paws cling to the bathtub.

Her claws come out, but there's nothing for them to grab.

She pulls. Her wet body heaves with effort. She grunts.

I'm so worried for her that I grunt and want to push her up.

She makes it!

I'm sure my grunting helped! (I'm SO involved with her story!)

She's on the bathtub's edge.

She throws back her head and crows her victory. "Owww!"

She shivers delicately and stops to lick her paw.

Now she shakes all over, slinging water everywhere.

She's a slicked-down, ugly cat.

(I'm sorry, PittyPat, but you look ugly when you're all wet.)

She hops down. Each foot lifts slowly, leaving a watery trail.

She takes a bite of her food.

Everything is silent. The music stops and waits.

Her first bite of food is crunchy.

Then comes the purring.

The big music comes back.

Success. Purr. Purr.

MY VIDEOS

What kind of stories do I want to tell with my acting?

I could fight and lose.

Fight and lose.

Fight and win.
A fight cat! That's what I want to be.
MamaGrace would never let me fight!
The Director would never let me fight!
Miss Tanya would never let me fight!

EPISODE 6
Ghost-Cat

— · ★ · —

The night is dark.
I hide behind a bush.
A girl is walking toward me.
I slink out in front of her.
She screams! "Ghost cat!"

The night is dark.
I hide behind a bush.
A boy and girl are skipping home.
I slink out in front of them.
They scream! "Ghost cat!"

No. This is all wrong.
I don't like slinking.
I don't like screams.
The video isn't telling a good story.
This is bad acting.

I'm not a good ghost cat.
I'm the right color.
But it doesn't show off my mixed eyes.
No.

TALK IT OUT
Decisions

=== ·★· ===

I stood outside the Director's office, shaking from head to tail.

Mr. Danny rolled his eyes and whispered, "He's in a bad mew-d. Good luck."

I shrugged. The Director had called me in, so I had to be here.

Mr. Danny motioned me inside.

The Director lay on a crimson pad, making his hairless skin look pink. The wrinkles on his neck rippled when he looked up at me.

I shook so hard that I was afraid I would fall down. Quickly, I sat on a white mat just in front of the Director.

"Ah, Angel," he said.

"Sir," I said.

"Angel, it's time to decide your future."

My head swam. Dizzy! "What do you mean?"

"You aren't a baby. You're a kitten. You can't be an innocent forever."

"No?"

"No." The Director leaned toward me. "You must decide. Or I'll decide for you."

He needed some purr-fume. His breath stank of anchovies, those salty, stinky canned fish. They were a delicacy, some said. But I hated them. I liked the peppermint-candy smell better.

"What are my choices?" I asked.

The Director threw a paw over his face and sighed.

Such acting! Why was he never on camera?

MamaGrace says that viewers want sweet cats. I was tired of being a sweet cat. Maybe viewers should try tough cats.

"You know your choices," the Director said. "Decide."

Behind the Director were screens. On each screen, a video was showing.

Water cats, dress-up cats, food cats, innocent cats, fat cats. Boring.

My eyes filled up with tears. But I did not cry. Miss Tanya would be mad if I cried.

"No," I said.

He looked up at the ceiling.

At his aquarium of goldfish that he kept for snacks. Out the window at the woods.

He sighed.

"Your sister is a great water cat," the Director said.

"No!" I said.

"Your brother is a great food cat," the Director said.

"No!" I said.

"We haven't had a piano cat for a long time," the Director said.

I thought about the white and black keys. "Maybe. But..."

He waited.

I thought about the fraidy-cat video.

I wanted to fight that falcon.

I wanted to be wild.

I wanted to fight and lose, fight and lose, fight and win.

I wanted to tell a video story about winning a fight. "What about a fight cat?" I asked.

The Director laughed.

His neck and stomach wrinkled and wrinkled. "You? A fight cat?"

And he laughed and laughed.

I hid my face under a paw.

But I did not cry.

Lights

=== · ★ · ===

STUDY: VIDEO LIGHTS

I needed to learn more about lights.

Lights are important for videos.

Without lights, details blur.

Without lights, a white coat might look gray.

Without lights, my eyes might look brown instead of blue and copper.

Lights can trick the viewer.

Soft, bright lights make a cat look happy.

Or make a cat look innocent.

A few hard lights make a cat look mean.

Or they can make a cat look like a fighter.

Ghost-cat videos only work if the light is right.

Innocent-cat videos only work if the light is right.

PittyPat likes hard light when she's swimming.

It looks like she's swimming strong.

But when she gets out of the water, wet cats look bad. She needs soft light to blur her image.

Quincy likes strong light.

"You need to see details of the food," he says.

They change the light when he starts eating.

"You need soft light for the meal," he says.

Lights can fool the viewer. They can make mean cats look innocent. Or innocent cats look like fight cats.

I needed to learn more about lights.

Hard lights.

EPISODE 7
Piano Cat

— · ★ · —

The Director had said, "We haven't had a piano cat for a long time."

Miss Tanya combed the hair on each paw.

Paws are important for a piano cat.

First I looked into the camera for a soul-connect.

Then I walked across the piano on the black keys.

At the end, I sang, "Me-me-meow!"

I walked back on the white keys.

At the end, I sang, "Me-me-meow!"

I had watched an old, old, old video of a piano cat.

She was mew-sical. She played a real song.

"Twinkle, Twinkle Little Star."

It was a hard song. But she didn't miss a note.

Then, she sang the whole song!

"Me-me-meow!" I said. "I can't be a piano cat. Too much singing." Besides, my singing was as sour as sour milk.

"Yowza," the Director said. "I have heard better singing."

TALK IT OUT
Dress-up Cat

=== · ★ · ===

The Director thinks I'm cute.

He told me to watch Jazz's videos. Maybe I could do cute videos like her.

Okay, I watched.

The Director is right. Jazz is cute.

She's feline-fine, the best dress-up cat in town.

JAZZ'S VIDEO 1

Snow drifted down.

Jazz made this video the same night that I'd made my snowflake video.

Jazz had sat like a doll. Her back feet stuck out in front.

She wore ski pants, a ski jacket, and a stocking hat.

She wore four mittens.

Jazz Snow Baby was cute.

JAZZ'S VIDEO 2

The blue pool glistened.

Jazz stood on her back legs. She held her front legs up in front of her body. She wore a red bikini.

She hopped, hopped, and then dived into the water.

Splash!

It was a mash-up video. It was part water cat and part dress-up cat.

Jazz Bikini Girl was cute.

She climbed out and put on a big floppy hat. Even wet, she was cute.

(Don't tell PittyPat I said that.)

Acting for a dress-up cat is a lot like acting for an innocent cat.

The dress-up cats don't move around very much.

They look at the camera a lot. Mostly, they just look cute.

NO! Not for me.

I'll tell Jazz that I love her work. And I do.

It's just not for me.

What I think does matter.

If I say NO, the Director will listen.

I think.

Roommates?

⸻ · ★ · ⸻

It was the fourth week of the Top Kitten competition, and we were ten weeks old. I pushed to the front to see the Director's list of top videos for the week. Someone shoved me hard. Looking around, Jazz was straining to read the list.

There it was. Top video of the week: Jazz's pirate video.

I'd seen that dress-up video and thought it was spectacular. Her costumes were amazing. Jazz was acting with great emotion too. It deserved to be the top video.

As usual, I was fourth. Quincy was eighth, and PittyPat was ninth. Filling in were kittens who had never been in the top ten before. The top ten videos each week always included Jazz, Quincy, PittyPat, and me. But after that, the spots were filled with random kittens who appeared in the top ten one time and didn't come back.

"Jazz," I said. "We need to talk."

She followed me to a quieter spot. Jazz's face was tight. I didn't know if she was worried about Top Kitten or something else. But I had to ask her anyway.

"Um," I said. "Next week, we turn ten weeks old."

"Yes, me too."

"That means we move into the kitten dormitory."

"Okay." Jazz raised an eyebrow.

She wasn't making this easy. "I wondered, you know, if you might...you know..." I waited.

"No, I don't know."

I blurted out, "Would you be my roommate in the dorm?"

For a moment, I was afraid that Jazz would laugh. Obviously, she was struggling with a strong emotion. Her jaw tightened, and her ears flattened.

Finally she said, "Why me?"

"Because I think we can be friends."

"What about the Top Kitten competition?"

"I think we could help each other," I said. "You challenge me to do my best. After I watch your videos, I try to think of new ways of acting."

Jazz spun around like she was chasing her tail. "Don't you care about winning? Or losing?"

I thought about losing. It would be the hardest thing I'd ever done. But by now, I knew I was out of the running. In the last four weeks, I'd never had the top video. Jazz had gotten the top video three times. Her family had hired Miss Emily Doodle to design and sew her costumes. Each outfit had a hat. The outfit covered only the front legs and chest. Miss Doodle sewed tiny human arms into the costume, so Jazz looked like a person from the front. She could attach things to the fake arms, like a sword, a hook for a pirate, or a guitar. It looked so realistic. Jazz had found a great niche for her videos.

She was bound to be Top Kitten. Could she put aside the competition and just be friends? Could I?

"Of course I care," I said. "But put it into perspective. It's a Top Kitten competition. Kitten. It's a big thing for us right now. But we won't be kittens forever."

Jazz's eyes were wide and scared. "I'm not sure I'm as nice as you. If I don't win Top Kitten..." She shook her head and looked back at the Director's office, where the list was posted.

"I can't give up trying to win, either. But we have to move to the dormitory next week. That leaves MamaGrace all alone. Watching videos of MamaGrace and DaddyAlbert, I can see what she's lost. She needs DaddyAlbert. If I make Top Kitten, I can bring him home."

Jazz turned back to me and nodded. "I understood that you have to keep trying. I'm just not sure I can be a friend no matter what."

"If you win, I'll celebrate with you. But inside, I'll be jealous," I said. "Just being honest."

"I'm not sure I could celebrate with you," Jazz said. "Just being honest."

"I'll take my chances. Maybe I know you better than you know yourself," I said. "Would you be my roommate?"

"We may regret this," she whispered. "Yes. Roommates. Friends."

EPISODE 8
Moving Day

=== · ★ · ===

The day before we turned ten weeks old was a beautiful but sad day. Tomorrow we'd move out of MamaGrace's apartment and into the dorms.

Quincy bounced up and down. "Tenth floor! Kitten dorm, here we come!"

I watched MamaGrace's face. Did her smile reach her eye? Was she happy about us moving out? "Where will you live now?" I asked.

"I'll take the small penthouse apartment. Come up and see me anytime." The top floor of Majestic Kennels had two penthouse apartments. Right now, we had the big one. The small one was only big enough for one cat.

"Will you work?" PittyPat asked.

"I'll never be in a video again." MamaGrace tapped the eye patch on her right eye. "But the

Director has asked me to do more acting lessons. I think I'll like that."

MamaGrace, I loved her so much. My heart was so full. But I couldn't find the right words. Even talkative PittyPat was silent.

MamaGrace didn't let us fuss, though. Instead, she said, "Let's go for a walk. Together."

We ran down the stairs and out into the warm summer day. We were together, as a family, one last time. As we were leaving Majestic Kennels, a cameraman followed us. We ignored him. They always follow the KittyTube stars in case something interesting happens. But they had orders not to video MamaGrace. The Director would make sure she was edited out of any video.

The air smelled of sweet roses. We followed MamaGrace with our tails held high, just as she'd taught us. We entered Central Park from the Broadway entrance. The curving path led around the park, our favorite walk.

First we stopped at our favorite statue. It was a bronze statue of Arlo Porter Wiles, the inventor of the cat-to-human speech translator. The statue showed Arlo seated on the ground, talking with three cats. MamaGrace had explained that Mr. Arlo Wiles had given the translator to the cats for free. He could've made a fortune on it. Instead, he gave it to the cat world. That's when cats started to take charge of their own lives and created KittyTube and the kennels.

MamaGrace said, "Albert loved this statue. The translator changed our lives."

We took turns jumping on the statue and pretending to talk with Mr. Arlo. Finally we continued our stroll around the park.

MamaGrace stopped to talk to another queen cat.

They talked and talked.

Bored, Quincy went around some bushes. He came back grinning and motioned for PittyPat and me to follow.

"Look!" He pointed to a mud puddle. Then he leaped into it and splashed us both.

PittyPat splish-splashed him back.

Miss Tanya would kill me! But this was my last day as a baby kitten. I ran for the puddle and slid through it, laughing.

Quincy laughed and then slid into the puddle. PittyPat rolled over in the puddle. Quincy pushed me, and I landed face-first.

"Stop!" MamaGrace stood over us. "Get out of that mud."

We lined up in front of MamaGrace, heads down.

I stared in horror at my muddy paws. What did my face look like? Miss Tanya…

MamaGrace paced back and forth in front of us. She didn't scold. But we knew we were in trouble.

I looked over MamaGrace's shoulder and saw the cameraman. He was only filming MamaGrace's left side. It wouldn't show her scar or the eye patch. So that was okay.

He was laughing. He saw me looking and gave me a thumbs-up.

I nudged Quincy and nodded toward the cameraman. He nudged PittyPat.

I giggled. Quincy giggled. PittyPat giggled. MamaGrace glanced at the cameraman. (She only turned her good side to the camera.) She looked back at us and shook her head.

She sighed.

But she smiled too.

Then loudmouth PittyPat was laughing. And MamaGrace laughed back.

The family laughed and hugged. We tugged MamaGrace until she was in the mud puddle too. That video—The Muddy Family—was MamaGrace's last video.

It's still one of my favorites.

It was our last day together as babies.

TALK IT OUT

A Mother-Daughter Chat

— • ★ • —

"Be yourself!" MamaGrace said. "Act like a dog."

It was my weekly acting lesson.

My tail swished on the carpet. MamaGrace's new penthouse room was comfortable. My dorm room only had wooden floors. There, my claws clinked when I walked. I liked MamaGrace's soft carpets.

"I'm not a dog!" I said. "How can I act like a dog and be myself?"

"No one else acts like you. You will do it differently. No one else will act like a dog in the same way. That's what the camera wants. You!"

"No," I said. "It wants a clean, quiet cat. The camera likes me when I sleep and yawn."

"What role do you want?"

"I want to fight. But I'm too small."

"I don't want you to get hurt. But as long as it's all acting, a fight cat would be interesting." MamaGrace tapped her eye patch. "It's not the size of the dog in the fight. It's the size of the fight in the dog. You'll find your way, Angel."

"Will I really?" I ached to be something new, something good.

"Yes," MamaGrace said. "It just takes time."

"Can I make up a new role?"

"Don't worry. We'll name the role you take on."

"What if I'm not good enough?"

"Every video cat wonders that. It's normal. Here's all I can say: Just be yourself, dear. You are enough."

"Are you enough, MamaGrace?" I studied her face. The smaller penthouse apartment suited her. It was large enough, but not too large. She'd hung dozens of photographs of herself and DaddyAlbert on the wall. "Are you happy now?"

She ran a paw over her face and stood up straighter. "I'm happy to teach acting. I never thought I'd like it, but it's fun. And I can do this for a long time."

She studied the photographs on the wall, her eyes moving from one to the next. And I knew she was thinking about DaddyAlbert.

I wanted DaddyAlbert to come home for MamaGrace's sake. But I also wondered what he'd think of my acting. Would he be proud of me? I was working hard to bring him home. But I also worked to live up to his example as an actor. I worked to make him proud of his daughter. But I was starting to doubt that I'd ever see DaddyAlbert.

"MamaGrace, is DaddyAlbert real?"

"Oh, Angel!"

"It's just that I don't know him. I only know that you love him."

"I understand." MamaGrace came to rub her shoulder against mine. Side by side, we looked at the photographs. "He's not been here," she said. "And when he gets here, he will have missed half your kittenhood. But know this: He loves you. If you ever need something, you can count on him. He'll have your back."

I nodded. "I hope so, MamaGrace. Quincy and PittyPat and I—we're trying to earn enough money to bring him home for you."

MamaGrace leaned forward, her nose touching mine. "It's okay, Angel. If you don't win Top Kitten, we'll figure out something. Albert is trying to find work too. Something will work out."

EPISODE 9
Surrender

===·★·===

The chicken saw me at the same time I saw it.

Squawk!

It was a pullet, a young chicken. I was just a young cat. It should've been a good match.

But the chicken didn't know that.

I had claws, good jumping, and good dodging.

The chicken had claws and a strong beak.

It leaped at me.

I twirled away and fell down.

The pullet jumped. It aimed its claws at me.

I rolled away. But that made me worry. My white coat would get dirty if I rolled a lot.

"Grrrowl!" I'd promised the Director that I'd stay clean.

The pullet struck out with its beak.

That was too close!

I didn't like this. It was too dangerous.

The pullet leaped again.

I rolled again.

The beak struck at me. Crazy chicken!

I rolled again.

"I surrender!" I screamed, "Cut! Cut! Cut!"

Surrender means "I give up."

A groomer rushed in and grabbed the pullet.

I looked down at my coat. The groomer stood there shaking his head.

It was going to take all day to get me white again.

The Director said nothing. He just flipped the switch, killing the lights. He didn't look at me.

He just walked away.

I dropped to the ground and cried.

I wasn't a dress-up cat.

I wasn't a water cat.

I wasn't a food cat.

I wasn't a fighter cat.

I was a nothing cat.

TALK IT OUT
A Director-Actress Chat

— · ★ · —

I sat in the Director's office on the white mat.

I wasn't shaking in fear. I was mad.

The Director said, "You'd be a great dress-up cat."

"No. I'd hate it. How do you act with a turban on? Or ballet shoes?"

He paced in front of me. "Then you'll keep on being a fraidy-cat. Everyone loves that."

"Except me. I want to be a Fight-cat," I said.

His eyes got big. His face wrinkled big. "Yowza. Fight what? Ferrets?"

A popular KittyTube video this week was "Ferret v. Cat." It featured Wesley Maine Coon, who was so big that the ferret didn't have a chance.

I shook my head. "No. I want a different kind of fight. Me against the world."

"Why?" the Director yelled. "You're adding wrinkles to my skin every day, Angel."

I knew what he thought.

I was white and couldn't get dirty.

I was small. My face was too sweet.

"Why not?" I asked.

Inside, I was quivering. But not outside. This time, I had to stand my ground. "It's opposite of what you expect. That's good. I'll surprise everyone."

"How? I don't even know how to do an 'Angel v. The World' video."

"We'll figure it out. Together," I said.

The Director raised his face to the sky and yowled, "Yowza!"

I hoped that meant I'd get to fight.

If we could figure out what that meant.

EPISODE 10
Dominoes
═ • ★ • ═

The mirrors said, "You look great."

I shivered and licked my fur. I had to look my best for a special group video.

Miss Tanya brushed the hair on my back.

"It's a simple trick," drawled Wesley Maine Coon. "We just stand there."

I knew the trick paws down. We'd worked on it three times in the mirror room. Wesley stood on one end, as the biggest cat. I stood at the other end, as the smallest cat. In between, the other cats stood in order of how big they were. Since she was a paw taller now, Jazz would stand beside me.

A red laser light came on. It moved all around the room.

We just watched the light.

Stand there. Watch the light.

That's all I had to do.

I reached my hind leg around and scratched under my chin. It was itchy today.

"Five minutes," called the Director. Today he smelled of peppermint candies. He wore a scarf around his scrawny neck.

Wesley said, "The Director has a cold. He'll be easy to please today."

I stretched. My ears twitched; I couldn't make them stop.

"Nervous?" Jazz asked. "It's a live audience, but you can't see the humans because they are behind the bright lights."

I just shrugged.

"Just ignore the lights," Jazz said. "Humans can't see very well without them, poor dears."

"Oh," I said. I always liked to know more about humans. After all, they were our viewers.

"Quiet on the set!" the Director called.

We joined the line of cats.

But I was itchy. I gave my tail a quick lick. Really, it was quite messy today.

Lights glared. I wanted to squint. But I had to keep my mixed eyes open.

One by one, we strolled onto the table.

Wesley went first. For this job, he only had to be tall. He looked like the king of the lions. The groomer had fluffed out his hair to look like a lion's mane. I liked how his legs were so straight and tall.

My ear itched. I tilted my head, but it still itched.

Next came Kathleen Ragdoll. She was a tricolor ragdoll. Her videos always got plenty of views.

Next came Daniel Siamese, Jazz's tall brother. Then Jazz walked onto the table.

Finally it was my turn. Slowly I walked onto the table and stood beside Jazz. I opened my eyes w-i-d-e. The camera looked at my mixed eyes.

From beyond the lights, I heard calls.

"Oh! That small one is so adorable."

"That big one is a monster!"

"Makes you want to pet them all."

My ear itched. I started to pull my hind leg out, but Jazz hissed out of the side of her mouth, "Not now!"

I tried to stand straight and tall, like Wesley.

But the ear itched.

The laser light came on. The others almost stood on tiptoe watching the red dot of light. It went right and left. I fought to be still. The team moved as one. We leaned right. We leaned left.

But I was off.

I needed to scratch.

Kathleen and Wesley and the Director glared at me.

I tried to ignore the itch.

Beside me, Jazz stood on tiptoe. She loved the red light. Her head turned to watch it.

I watched the red light too. I liked the red light. Really. But—

—my hind leg reached out by itself. It scratched my ear.

But it didn't reach my ear.

Instead, my leg bumped Jazz.

Just a teensy tiny bit. Really. But Jazz fell.

When Jazz fell, she knocked into Daniel.

Daniel pushed over Kathleen.

Kathleen slammed into Wesley.

Wesley. Big, sweet Wesley.

He wavered. He tried to catch himself.

For a moment, I thought he'd stand firm.

But then he tumbled, head over heels.

Of course, he landed on his feet. Even kittens know how to do that.

The live audience was silent. Shock.

Then the laughter started in low. And it started to grow.

Wild laughter. Ha, ha, ha, ha, ha, ha, ha, ha, ha, ha, ha!

"Domino cats!" yelled someone.

The live audience loved it!

Wesley did not love it.

He leaped up beside me. He towered over me.

I shrank down.

Wesley growled deep in his chest. "Grrrow!"

I thought the Director would call, "Cut!" But the film kept rolling.

Wesley turned slowly. He looked at the camera. He stood like the king of the beasts. He was in control of his everything.

He glared down at me. I was just an ant in his path. He smiled a wide cat smile for the camera. Bending low, he faked licking me.

He growled in my ear, "If you ever do that again…"

I gulped.

But Jazz was there, talking in my other ear. "Angel! Be a fight cat."

So then I got mad.

No. I wasn't a fraidy-cat any longer.

MamaGrace's words echoed in my mind: It's not the size of the dog in the fight, it's the size of the fight in the dog.

I growled back. "Grrrow!"

I reared up on my hind legs. I swatted at Wesley's face.

He pulled back. And fell.

Boom!

Instantly, he was on his feet again.

"Yowza," said the Director. "A disaster."

But MamaGrace said quietly, "Underdog cat."

As usual, MamaGrace had it right. They edited a separate video of me fighting with Wesley. It went viral.

I was the new underdog cat. A totally new role for cats, created just for me. And my viewers.

And the viewers clicked.

And clicked.

And clicked.

And clicked.

KA-ching!

Top Kitten

— ⋅★⋅ —

Stage 9, Majestic Kennels' largest soundstage, was the best stage in Kittywood. Albert Persian usually taped on Stage 9. Some of the biggest hits had been filmed on Stage 9.

On a sunny Saturday morning, the twenty-seven kittens in the Top Kitten competition crowded into the Stage 9's greenroom. That's the room where actors waited for their turn to be filmed. We were all weaned and living in dorms, so no mothers were allowed.

Wide open, Stage 9 was an adaptable space with the best lights possible. A blank canvas, the Director could create anything on Stage 9.

Today the Director would announce who was the Top Kitten. And then we'd all stay to film the public service announcement, or PSA, about Kitten Adoption Month. A PSA is a message in the public interest that is broadcast free. It might look like an advertisement. But the message is meant to raise public awareness about an issue. Our message would be to adopt a kitten.

The only human in the greenroom was a short groomer. She sat on a stool, guarding the door to Stage 9. She smelled like rose-scented shampoo.

"Quiet," she called.

But meows filled the room.

Jazz and I walked around, saying hello to everyone.

One ragdoll kitten chased his tail. He stopped, licked a paw, and said to no one, "Don't you love Flash Feline? He's so fast. I never get tired of watching him chase his tail."

I tilted my head and tried to remember. "Does he ever catch it? By the way, I'm Angel. This is Jazz."

"Everyone knows you two," he said. "I'm Kirk."

My eyebrows went together in confusion. "Everyone knows us?"

"Jazz is probably Top Kitten. And you're in the top five. Of course everyone knows you."

Jazz's eyes were shining with hope. "I can't add up all the numbers. But I did have the top video of the week for four weeks straight."

I didn't answer. I couldn't add the numbers either. But I'd never had a top video. I couldn't possibly win. And yet I still hoped that the numbers would surprise me. Foolish.

Suddenly the door flung open. The Director filled the doorway. His large ears pointed upward. He came into Stage 9's greenroom, followed by MamaGrace.

At one end of the room was a tiny stage. They both stepped onto it so everyone could see them.

"It's time to announce the winners of the KittyTube competition," the Director said.

Pandemonium broke out. The clowder of kittens meowed, squeaked, and yowled. By now, most of the twenty-seven kittens knew they couldn't win—just like me. But they still yelled, "Top Kitten! That's me!"

Watching, sadness weighed me down. It was like I had ten turtle shells on my back. I moved slowly. Quincy, PittyPat, and I hadn't done enough. DaddyAlbert wouldn't come home. On the stage, MamaGrace kept her face down. She knew the truth too.

The Director said, "Third place goes to Quincy Persian."

PittyPat and I grabbed each other and spun in circles.

Quincy proudly strode to the front and stood beside MamaGrace and the Director.

"The first- and second-place winners were both amazing. In fact, there were only ten views separating first place from second place."

The kittens said, "Oooh!"

"It was almost a tie."

"Oooh!"

"The second-place winner never had a top video of the week. But overall, she was consistently in the top five. Second place goes to Angel Persian."

I was stunned. My views were the most consistent? I was only ten views short of first place?

PittyPat was squealing. "We did it! Second place is $500. And Quincy wins $250 for third place. That's enough. It's enough for DaddyAlbert to come home."

Joy filled my heart, and Stage 9 seemed to blaze with golden light. We'd done it. DaddyAlbert could come home.

In a daze, I stood beside my mother and brother on the stage. In a daze, I heard the Director announce that Jazz was Top Kitten. But it didn't matter. Together, Quincy and I had done it.

After the announcements, everyone milled around for a while. I found Jazz to congratulate her. Because Jazz was Top Kitten, the Director had invited her parents to be there.

When I walked up, Jazz's mother was talking. "I knew you'd make it," she said. "I'm so proud of you."

Jazz hiccupped, and then tears ran down her cheeks.

Joy filled me again that Jazz had won.

I introduced myself to Jazz's family. "I'm Angel Persian."

Mrs. Siamese's eyes were large and dark. "Oh, I'm glad to meet you. Jazz talks about you all the time."

I was only ten views away from being Top Kitten. But I felt like a Top Kitten. I had a good friend, along with $500 in the bank, and MamaGrace was happier than I'd ever seen her. DaddyAlbert would come home soon.

"But look out," I told Jazz. "When there's another competition, I'll be out to win."

"Yeah. And you might win the next one," Jazz said. "After all, you're the underdog cat."

Finally the Director called, "Time to film the PSA." He led everyone out onto Stage 9. For one last time, under the soft lights, we kittens would be innocents. We'd be helpless kittens calling out for someone to give us a home.

The Director called out stage directions. "Jazz! Get up here."

She would lead the line of kittens for the PSA.

"Angel and Quincy, as second- and third-place winners, you'll be right behind Jazz."

My tail wobbled with excitement as I walked to my position.

"Now," the Director said, "I want the pale coats next. Then tricolors. Deep-colored coats last. You only have to do one thing. Heads up. Eyes at the camera. Walk slowly."

That sounded easy.

The Director turned away, then whirled back. "Oh, one more thing. No one get ahead of Jazz. Stay a step behind her. She's Top Kitten."

Walking behind Jazz, I realized I was truly happy for her. Her goal had always been Top Kitten. My goal had always been to bring DaddyAlbert home, and we had enough money for that. We had both won.

The Director told us, "When Jazz gets to her X, then everyone stops. She'll meow, sad and lonely. Then everyone will join in."

"Action!" called the Director.

We strolled forward with our heads up. I walked straight ahead. Even though I wasn't Top Kitten, I did the soul-connect thing with the camera. Behind me, the Kittywood kittens marched in step.

We marched until Jazz found her X-marks-the-spot. We stood in ranks behind her.

It was Jazz's moment. "Mew, mew, mew." She gave a quiet plea for help. "Meow. Eh!"

Please, people, adopt a kitten. See how gentle and helpless we are. We need your help.

We joined in, a chorus of kittens pleading for a home. "Meow."

"Cut," called the Director. "Yowza! Great job!"

The kittens crowded around Jazz, congratulating her.

A few minutes later, the Director called into the speaker, "We have one more thing to do. Angel, Quincy, and PittyPat, come up here."

Quincy raised an eyebrow as a question, and PittyPat was hard to tear away from her friends. Finally we stood beside the Director.

"I have a surprise for you," the Director said.

From somewhere, music blared. It was grand-entrance music. An entrance is when an actor or actress first comes into a story. A spotlight flashed on the side door to Stage 9. It opened.

There stood a tortoiseshell Persian cat with a red and golden coat. He had golden eyes, golden eyebrows, a golden chin and a lovely gold streak down his face. He looked exactly as MamaGrace had described him.

DaddyAlbert.

My heart banged so hard, my chest hurt.

MamaGrace dashed across the empty space to DaddyAlbert, and they embraced. Quincy knocked my head and bumped PittyPat with his shoulder. Then we ran to meet our daddy.

He looked up. We stopped, not sure what to do.

DaddyAlbert spoke with a deep, rich voice. "You must be PittyPat."

She stepped forward, eager, and he crushed her against his chest.

"I've been watching you swim," DaddyAlbert said. "You really pull the audience in. Great job!"

PittyPat beamed.

I wondered if he'd watched any of my videos. Most of them were innocent roles. Would he think that I needed to grow up more?

"And you're Quincy."

Quincy stepped forward and held out a paw to shake. But DaddyAlbert pulled him into a bear hug.

"You're the bravest cat I've ever seen," DaddyAlbert said. "I'd never eat a spider like that."

Quincy puffed out his chest and grinned up at DaddyAlbert.

MamaGrace was watching, her eye glittering, as if tears would fall at any moment.

I worried. Did DaddyAlbert watch any of my videos?

Finally he turned to me. "Angel. The white beauty with the odd eyes."

I stepped forward, uncertain and shaky.

His golden eyes fixed me with a steady gaze. "I've been watching your videos."

I gulped. My heart thumped loudly in my ears. What would he think of my acting?

"Here's the thing," DaddyAlbert said. "You started out good. But with every video, your acting has gotten better and better."

Eagerly, I said, "I watched your old videos. I tried to do everything like you."

He nodded solemnly. "Yes, I could tell. I'm so proud of you."

We stared at each other while my heart swelled. All the work, all the study, all the trying so hard—DaddyAlbert was proud of me. I closed my eyes against the tears. Proud. Of me.

"Come here, daughter," DaddyAlbert said.

Suddenly we were hugging. He smelled like spices and sugar. When I leaned into him, his voice rumbled and echoed around in my chest.

DaddyAlbert turned and pulled in the whole family. "PittyPat. Quincy. Angel. Grace. Finally."

DaddyAlbert was home.

The Golden Family

— • ★ • —

Of course they videotaped the Persian family reunion (making sure to only shoot MamaGrace's good side). It's been the top video for three weeks straight. Everyone expects it to set records. We are, after all, the Golden Family.

THE END

If you enjoyed this book,

please consider leaving a review!

Find more information about the video cats at

Mimshouse.com/video-cats

Read more by
DARCY PATTISON

THE ALIENS, INC. SERIES

Book 1: Kell, the Alien

Book 2: Kell and the Horse Apple Parade

Book 3: Kell and the Giants

Book 4: Kell and the Detectives

Made in United States
Orlando, FL
06 January 2022